The Dolphin and

How to Sell More Faster
with
Sales Process Engineering

By Todd Youngblood
Managing Partner & CEO
The YPS Group, Inc.
www.ypsgroup.com

Published by
The YPS Group, Inc.
Acworth, GA 30101
www.ypsgroup.com

Acknowledgements

Until I decided to write this book, I did not really appreciate how much of what I know is really only the reflected wisdom of colleagues, friends and the business people I have worked with throughout my career. It has been a humbling experience.

A few people really stand out…

❖ Rick Howe, President of The Knotts Company – The YPS Group's first real customer, long time friend, the world's best sounding board and someone who genuinely cares about and celebrates my success.

❖ Jack Katzbach – the most respected sales manager I have ever known; he has proven that nice guys really can be extraordinary winners.

❖ Joe Zielinski – who always listens patiently and attentively to every business brainstorm that crashes into my head …and then makes it better.

❖ Charlie Aimone – my first sales manager; I've followed his advice for so long that I think the ideas are my own.

Finally, I must thank my wife, Marilyn. With two sets of college tuition payments looming, she supported my move away from the very secure world of "Corporate America" so that I could chase my dreams.

Preface

The Dolphin and the Cow?

Somehow, a memorable metaphor always
seems to help me remember core concepts.
For better or for worse, I assume that most
readers of this book will agree.

The "sales" dolphin shown here represents the
traditional, first-rate selling professional -
graceful, effortlessly quick, a thing of beauty
to watch! But, as we all know, the world has
changed and the pace of that change continues
to accelerate. We are all too familiar with

how the "dot.com" boom become a "dot.bomb," but not before it permanently and profoundly altered the business world.

The industrial sector has been contracting and will continue to shrink as a percentage of GDP. According to a recent study by Alliance Capital Management, factory employment in the U.S. declined 11% from 1995 to 2002. Most of us are just beginning to realize, however, that something more is happening. That same study also points out a 20% decline in Brazil, a 16% decline in Japan and a 15% decline in China. So I guess our jobs really *aren't* just being exported overseas… Something even more fundamental must be going on.

The point here (and the point of this entire book) is that **the "sales dolphin" can no longer swim alone.** A new and different sort of help is needed. Things like metrics, statistical analysis and control and Sales Process Engineering or "SPE" are becoming more and more essential.

In the 19th century, these disciplines were applied to agriculture. That is why we no longer need 80% of the population to grow food. Since the 1940s, manufacturing executives have been applying them. That is why factory employment is dropping dramatically world-wide. Sales executives are next.

Teaching the "SPE Cows" to swim with the "Sales Dolphins" will become *the* competitive differentiator for a sales force. Read on. I trust that what follows will help.

The Dolphin and the Cow

**Sell More Faster
with
Sales Process Engineering**

Table of Contents

Chapter 1 - Introduction

A fundamental assumption...

All professional sales reps, managers and executives are committed to the relentless pursuit of excellence.

Unfortunately, this statement does not apply universally. Even a less ambitious assumption - that all are committed to sustaining continuous improvement - might well be too aggressive. Be that as it may... Those who genuinely embrace either form of this outlook will find the greatest value in this book and its underlying Sales Process Engineering principles.

There is another key factor inherent in this assumption. That is the need for relentless, never-ending, methodical discipline. Discipline in critically and formally analyzing the weaknesses in your sales process and its execution is essential. The more discipline one can muster and maintain, the greater the value of these results and principles.

Please take the paragraphs above seriously. There are no silver bullets or quick fixes presented here. Be prepared to move outside your intellectual comfort zone. Those who do will be both humbled and energized by the potential for sales performance enhancement that's out there.

The Need for Metrics

Most sales managers measure the effectiveness of their reps based on a single number - revenue production. Clearly, that is *the* key metric. By itself, however, it is woefully inadequate as a comprehensive management tool. Many sales managers, use 4 or 5 metrics, including things like calls made, proposals submitted, profitability and growth rate. A few use as many as a dozen or more. So, how many metrics of sales performance is optimal? Fundamentally, the answer is, "more than you have now." Consider the following scenario…

You have just "volunteered" to manage a little league baseball team. Maybe you played the game yourself at age 10 or so, but assume that for the most part, you really have no idea what to do. (By the way, even if you really do know little or nothing about the game, the analogy will still be quite clear.)

One of your first tasks will be to decide on the batting order, the sequence in which the kids will step up to the plate and attempt to hit the ball. Having no metrics at all, a random decision is the only choice. That is, the success of your first management decision will be based purely on luck.

Change the scenario. Add a metric. Assume that you find a listing of last year's batting average for each kid on the team. Now you know the percentage of time that each batter is likely to get a hit. You can now make a better batting order decision. One sensible approach would be to put the kid with the highest average first, the second highest, next, etc. That way, the best hitters have a greater chance at getting more turns at bat. Other approaches - *based on your data* – could also make sense. The point is, your decision is no longer random. Success in no longer based purely on luck.

Change the scenario again. Add a second metric. Assume you also find the percentage of time each kid actually got on base last year. (This is different than batting average. In addition to actually getting a hit, a batter can get on base by drawing a walk, getting hit by a pitch, or due to error made by a fielder on the other team.) You can now make an even better batting order decision. For example, put the kids with the three highest on-base percentages up to the plate first, second and third. Put the kid with the highest batting average up fourth. Doing so increases the odds that your best hitter will go to bat with three runners on base, thus increasing your odds of scoring more runs. One metric yields a better decision than no metrics. Two metrics yield a better decision than one.

The scenario can continue to change. What if you also knew each player's stolen base percentage, runs-batted-in, extra-base-hit percentage… *Each additional metric enhances the manager's ability to make a better decision.*

Now shift gears from your local Little League. How many metrics does a ***real*** baseball manager use? Major League

Baseball's web site (www.mlb.com) lists 109 distinct measurements of individual performance. (109!!!) Since both individual *and* team metrics are important, it's really twice that, or 218. Also, in the real world, they consider right-handed and left-handed pitching, so it's 436. Then you have day games and night games - 872. Then there are those other measurements that aren't published on the web site... Then there's X... Then there's Y... You get the picture.

Big league baseball managers use literally thousands of metrics, along with the possible combinations and permutations. They do so because they are committed to excellence. They do so because their competition is tough. ***They do so because each additional metric enhances their ability to make good management decisions***. Metrics help them predict what is most likely to happen on the next pitch, which in turn enables them to maximize the odds of having the right player in the right place at the right time, anticipating the right thing.

To further reinforce the point, consider Major League Baseball's Oakland Athletics. Since 1998, they have been extremely aggressive in applying process engineering and statistical analysis to winning baseball games on a tight budget. Their total budget for player salaries is less than 1/3 that of the New York Yankees. ($57 million vs. $180 million) In 1999, Oakland ranked 11th of 14 in the American League in terms of total salaries paid to players and 5th in the number of games won. In 2000 they were 12th in salary paid and 2nd in wins. In 2001, 12th and 2nd again. In 2002, 12th in salary, but 1st in wins. In 2003, 12th in salary, 2nd in wins. The Yankees spent roughly $1.8 million for each of their wins. Oakland spent less than $600 thousand.

Not only does extensive, aggressive use of metrics produce excellent results, it also dramatically decreases the investment required to do so.

So back to the original question… How many metrics of sales performance really *is* optimal? Same answer as before, *"More than you have now."* Every additional metric enhances the sales manager's ability to make better decisions.

Focus on process!

People execute processes to produce results. Achieving consistent good results is more dependent on the process than on the individual executing it. In fact, the process is *far* more important.

If you get nothing else from this book, get that point.

Consider Henry Ford for a moment. Undoubtedly, he was a genius. He built his first vehicles by himself, assembling them one piece at a time. Having invented and produced a viable, low-priced car, he had two choices. He could either focus on people (by hiring and training high-priced folks with the wherewithal to imitate his own craft), or he could *focus on the process* of building cars (by thoroughly understanding, documenting and continuously improving his know-how).

His pool of potential talent for option one numbered - at most - in the hundreds. For option two it numbered in the tens of thousands. Henry chose option two. The result was an assembly line-based car production process and the ability to manufacture a massive quantity of high-quality cars at a reasonable cost. Further, he worked very diligently to create a legacy of capturing the flashes of brilliance from his employees, incorporating the flashes into the existing process and creating a cycle of continuous improvement.

Henry Ford became a household name because he focused on process.

Dell was a relative latecomer to the PC business. Today, Dell is one of a very few top-tier providers of PCs. Oddly, Dell is not at all proficient at building PCs. "Youngblood", you say, "How can this be?" It is so because Dell focused on and got to be world class at a more relevant *process* than did its competitors.

If you happen to use a Dell, do you care that it was not built by them, but probably by SCI in Huntsville, AL? Of course not. You *do* care about how easy Dell made the process of configuring, ordering and getting delivery of the right hardware and software to the right knowledge worker at the right time.

Michael Dell became a household name because he focused on process.

The same focus-on-process concept holds true for any business, public sector, personal, artistic, athletic, individual or group process you can name. Take a minute and think about it.

While you're thinking, notice a subtle difference between the two examples above. In the early 1800s, the idea of focusing on process at all was enough to create a huge competitive advantage that lasted for many years. In the late 1900s, it took a focus on the *appropriate* process that created marketplace leadership.

People are still important

Good, well-trained employees are still required to achieve success. Continue to read the self-improvement books. Continue to focus on learning more and more and more about sales techniques and tools. Continue to push your team to become a true "learning organization". As an individual, learn all there is to learn. The more you know, the more successful you will become.

Just remember that the greatest sales rep in the world, using a poor sales process, will not progress beyond production of mediocre results. Conversely, an average rep can break the bank by using a superior sales process.

People are still important, but it is good process that creates the real leverage.

Sales is a process

The goal of this book is to help you and your company to sell more faster. The strategy to do so is to provide a roadmap to get you started down the path of Sales Process Engineering. Sales is a process. It is far more than a polished, professional sales call delivered by a product/service expert who also understands the prospect's needs, potential applications, industry and internal operations. (…not that you don't need all that…)

Sales is a process, just like manufacturing, distribution, financial management and purchasing are processes. The traditional rep who wants to be given product/service training, a few brochures and then to be left alone is a thing of the past.

Like any other process, an in-depth understanding of your sales process is essential. Like any other process, its linkages to other internal and external processes must be understood.

Creative Discipline

Think about those two words for a minute… Think about how they represent conflicting concepts.

Creativity - the hallmark of the right-brained free spirit; freedom from the constraints of bureaucracy; independence; the ability to see and articulate the big new picture. Without it there is no progress.

Discipline – the hallmark of the left-brained engineer; methodical execution of the scientific method; adherence to mathematical standards; control; the ability to repeatedly produce identical results. Without it there is no progress.

The fact is, both creativity and discipline are pre-requisites for progress. One without the other simply does not work. All of the heroes in history - be it philosophy, government, sports, music, inventing, politics, the military or business – demonstrated "Creative Discipline."

Most of you reading this book are in a sales role. Most likely your DNA makes you very comfortable with doing creative work. That's why most people get into sales to begin with. For us sales types, however, the discipline stuff is not so comfortable. Rules and procedures cramp our styles and seem to interfere with our effectiveness. Down deep though, we understand the need for repeatability, and appreciate the value of discipline.

For that reason, the focus of this book is on the discipline side of the coin. Not that the creative side is unimportant. Quite the contrary; it is essential. Much, however, has already been written about the creative, "dolphin-like" aspects of sales discussed in the preface. There is not too much that addresses the need for "cow-like" discipline.

Chapter 2 - Why Does Sales Process Engineering work?

A well-executed Sales Process Engineering effort inevitably creates a powerful cycle of improvement in sales productivity. Typically, an 8-12% annual increase in sales performance per rep results – and that's the result of the process alone. It's above and beyond any additional revenue growth enhancements due to new products, a generally strong economy or other external factors. You might think of this phenomenon as the "SPE Effect".

In any sales force, the performance of individual sales reps varies. A classic "bell curve" results by graphing the number of reps against sales dollars produced per rep. The sales volume of the best few reps will usually be about twice that of the lowest performers. The bulk of the sales team falls into a mid-range. This situation is represented by the first curve labeled "Start" below.

The "SPE" Effect

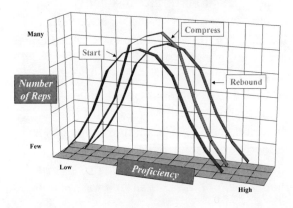

The impact of a Sales Process Engineering effort initially emerges as enhanced performance at the low end. This is due to disciplined "capturing", documentation, communication and implementation of the sales practices of the eagles by the low-end reps. The second curve labeled "Compress" above illustrates the two things that occur. First, the total range of productivity narrows. Second, as shown by the higher peak, a greater number of reps begin to perform at around the average productivity rate.

Most managers have had the pleasure of watching a star performer instinctively react to a challenge of his or her superior skills. This caliber individual simply will not stand for a ranking that is drifting toward the middle of the pack. He or she is self-compelled to maintain an edge. The result is shown mathematically by the third "Rebound" curve. The natural range of productivity and normal shape of the curve is relentlessly restored by your eagles - - - *at a higher level of total production for the entire sales force.*

Although the above explanation uses "Sales Per Rep" to illustrate the range of skills in a sales force, keep in mind that this is far from the only applicable metric. Proficiency at any and all specific sales skills can and must also be similarly tracked and graphed. For example, ability to identify potential opportunities, ability to schedule the first face-to-face appointment, customer knowledge, product knowledge, proposal writing and closing could also be used. Whatever skill you measure will produce the same bell curve, but different reps will fall into the weak, average and strong categories for each one. Each rep, therefore, learns from every other rep as total performance improves.

This brings us to a critical and quite counter-intuitive point... *Focus on getting all sales reps to at least an average level of performance on all key skills.* (Re-read the last sentence three times!)

Some explanation is in order. Being among the best at anything is really difficult. The sales leader who can propel all reps to an "excellent" rating for all skills is rare, in fact, non-existent. On the other hand, most sales leaders can get folks to "average." ***It is not <u>you</u> who drives the eagles to excellence.*** It is the nature of the beast that does the trick. Your focus needs to be on getting the laggards up to average in all key skills. This is the engine that drives the eagles. They will set the "excellence" bar higher without any prompting from management, which by default sets the "average" bar higher and starts this virtuous cycle all over again.

The final point in this section will probably strike you as obvious, but it must be emphasized. Never-ending persistence is essential. Now and then you will get lucky and have a large burst of improvement. Great! Virtually all progress, however, comes in baby steps. Given that, you have to stay at it forever. As my partner Cornell Wright often says, "Gentle pressure relentlessly applied," is the real key.

Chapter 3 - Process Maturity

Because process is paramount, it is critical to understand its nature. An appreciation of process maturity is fundamentally important. Think about it as a progression through five levels – Instinctive, Repetitive, Methodical, Measured and Systemic.

Sales Process Maturity

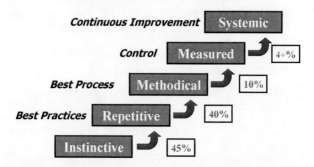

Maturity Level 1: Instinctive

In my sales training classes, I always ask how many of the women who as children had subjected their fathers to the output of an "Easy-Bake" oven. That question is followed by taking a headcount of the number of fathers who at least one time enthusiastically, if not totally honestly, endorsed the high quality and fine taste of those awful little cookies. I also ask them to recall the first time they (tried to) hit a golf ball, jump rope, play a musical instrument, etc.

There seems to be universal agreement that the only way to achieve success as a beginner at anything is to work incredibly hard or to be incredibly lucky.

Recall your very first sales call… In fact, remember those first few months… Bring back as many of the details as possible. How comfortable were you? How confident did you feel?

More than likely, your early successes were due mainly to determination, hard work and your gut instincts. You, like every other rookie rep, started out at this *instinctive* level of sales process maturity.

Our research indicates that roughly 45% of sales reps are at this level.

Maturity Level 2: Repetitive

To continue the cooking process analogy, I recall when my older daughter began to prepare meals that the family actually enjoyed. For whatever reason, she became intrigued with feeding us and consciously observed how others did it. She watched TV cooking shows, asked a lot of questions and experimented with her own ideas. In business terms, she began collecting best practices.

The same type of story could be told with regard to golf, musical instruments or selling. As time passed in your career, you were astute enough to recognize that some sales techniques and tactics worked better than others. Like any "maturing" rep, you consciously focused on executing the tasks that consistently produced results. You moved up to the *repetitive* level of sales process maturity. Perhaps without consciously knowing it, you became a student of "Sales Best Practices." You not only repeated the things that worked for you, but studied others and emulated the things that worked for them and continued to experiment.

Our research indicates that nearly 40% of sales reps are at this level.

Maturity Level 3: Methodical

One more time with the cooking analogy… Anyone who has prepared and served a traditional American Thanksgiving dinner shares an insight. The turkey might be perfect, along with the stuffing, sweet potatoes, gravy, etc. The real problem is timing. Not only does each component of the meal require cooking best practices for consistent, high quality results, but also its preparation must be coordinated with that of every other component. The more courses and the more dishes per course, the more complex and challenging it becomes to provide the perfect dining experience. (Who wants cold turkey with hot potatoes and reheated vegetables?)

While most cookbooks are excellent collections of "Cooking Best Practices," their focus is component by component. Very few have gone the extra - quite difficult - mile of documenting the exact optimum sequence and timing of tasks starting with the shopping trip, through preparation, serving, cleanup and effective, creative use and consumption of leftovers.

Similarly, not many companies have their sales best practices documented and readily available for pragmatic use. (Strictly speaking that's the requirement for Level 2.) Still fewer have invested the time and made the - again, quite difficult - effort to write down the entire sequence and timing of events that consistently leads to superior sales performance. In addition to the list of steps, the sales process also needs to be flow-charted. The "picture" a flow chart provides, aids and accelerates understanding and greatly simplifies the identification of dependencies on others, redundancies and/or unnecessary steps. (See Appendix IV.)

If you have never tried to document your complete sales process, doing so may sound simple. It's not. In fact, most are amazed at how difficult it is. Perhaps even more surprising ("upsetting" may be a better word) is how little agreement there is as to what the process actually entails. I repeat –

documenting a sales process will turn out to be much tougher than you think.

Don't kid yourself! I make a habit of asking sales executives if they have a sales process. Virtually always, the reply is a confident, "Yes." Next I ask if I could see a copy. Almost always I see a jolt in their eyes and then get a speech about how "all the reps know it." The dust on the cover chagrins even those few that can actually produce a copy.

A "Sales Best Process" has a profound superiority over a collection of "Sales Best Practices."

Our research shows that only about 10% of sales reps/organizations ever move up to this *methodical* level.

Maturity Level 4: Measured

Keep score and track statistics about everything. Level 4 implies tracking far more than number of calls made, proposals in process, revenue year-to-date and backlog. Some level 4 firms record, track and report on the quality and quantity of as many as fifty unique sales tasks.

If that strikes you as excessive, consider for a moment a different business process – manufacturing. Any plant manager of even a small facility can produce data regarding quantity, quality, speed, temperature, pressure, length, width, height, weight, cost and time. Not only that, reports on each of these data points, their relationships to each other and trends can be produced for at least each day of operations, probably for each hour and in some cases for much smaller units of time. In other words, they keep and regularly and effectively use thousands of real time statistics.

Statistical Process Control (SPC) is **the** key enabler of profitable manufacturing operations. Statistical Process Control is also **the** key enabler of profitable sales operations.

Some of you are thinking, "No, no, no – the sales process is very different from the manufacturing process." Every sales situation is unique. Sales reps need to be free to do whatever it takes. Sales requires constant adaptation and adjustment.

Consider this… Before the Model T's introduction in 1908, every car made was – literally - unique. The people building those cars were professionals, free to adapt and adjust as needed to complete the job. (Just like your sales reps?)

Before 1908, only the wealthy could afford a car. But then, Mr. Ford started to focus on process. He implemented some rudimentary statistical control over his process and became a legend. Hundreds of other "wanna-be" auto tycoons got driven into bankruptcy.

After World War II, Japanese car manufacturers very nearly totally overwhelmed their U.S. counterparts. They listened carefully to W. Edwards Deming and others (mostly Americans!) who advocated "SPC" (Statistical Process Control).

I wonder if any of your competitors has been carefully measuring and monitoring their sales process and is about to unleash the selling equivalent of a Model T or Toyota Corolla?

Our research indicates that less than 5% of sales organizations have legitimately reached this *measured* level.

Maturity Level 5: Systemic

According to our definition, a level 5 sales force has implemented an automated, monitored, simple-to-use, painless, self-tuning, self-correcting sales process that has feedback loops for each significant sales activity and *never* fails.

Quite frankly, we have yet to find anyone who meets those criteria. If they're out there, they're surely not talking much about it.

What's really troubling is this… Many, many sales execs are expending considerable time, money and resources to implement Customer Relationship Management (CRM) and Sales Force Automation (SFA) systems. Legitimately, these efforts are squarely aimed at "Level 5". To date, something like 70% of these projects have failed. Ouch!

The explanation for such a high failure rate is really quite simple. Successful sales people, managers and execs are universally positive, self-confident, aggressive and striving to be number one. Aim high! Go for Level 5! Here's the rub. Before my CRM system can provide *meaningful* statistical analysis, I must know what the key indicators are. That is, I need to be a black–belt Level 4. Before I can even measure more than a handful of sales activities, I must have my sales process defined in detail. That is, I need to be a black-belt Level 3. Before I can hope to define a sales process that is *consistently used by my entire sales force*, I must have a deep, visceral understanding of my Sales Best Practices. (Note that it's not "useful", "helpful" or "good" practices, but truly "Best.") To get to be this Level 2 black-belt, I need to have expended substantial, genuine, long-term effort to collecting, codifying and organizing all those little things that work.

Simply put, the laws of nature won't let your sales team skip a level. **Note the words "sales team"**. Just because you, the sales leader, are ready for the leap to Level 3, does not mean that the bulk of the sales team is ready. CRM and SFA projects fail to produce the desired results because the decision makers fail to do the requisite level 2, 3 and 4 "heavy lifting."

Key Constraints and Sub-Processes

Unless you have a hard-core engineer's genetic code, the idea of taking your entire sales team and entire sales process methodically through each maturity level is not particularly appealing. Unless you have lots of idle cash and a comfortable, sustainable lead on all of your competitors, it is also far too risky.

Break it down into parts. Identify THE key constraint, bottleneck, most common obstacle to closing deals. Focus on the sub-processes, the components of your complete sales process that address that constraint. Move up a maturity level or two with those activities – until that factor is no longer the most significant obstacle. Then go identify the *new* "key constraint" and repeat the process over and over and over. Baby steps!

"TODOs"

1) Rate the maturity or your overall sales process on three levels on a quarterly basis.

   a) In regard to yourself, personally
   b) In regard to the sales team or teams that report to you
   c) In regard to your entire company

2) List the top 10 activities/skills that contribute the most to your personal success.

   a) Put them in priority sequence
   b) Rate your maturity level for each of these 10 skills
   c) Develop and implement a plan to raise the level of three of these activities/skills in the next 90 days

3) Repeat step two with regard to the sales team or teams that report to you

4) Repeat step two with respect to your whole company

5) Track your progress on all of the above for the next ten years. (NOTE: Your top ten list will change over time as new key constraints present themselves. That's OK. You only have a problem if the list never changes!)

Chapter 4 - The Process of Sales Process Engineering

A well-executed Sales Process Engineering initiative can generate an 8-12% annual, incremental increase in sales performance per sales rep. As noted earlier, this is above and beyond the impact of new products and services, a strong economy, etc.

**The Process of
Sales Process Engineering**

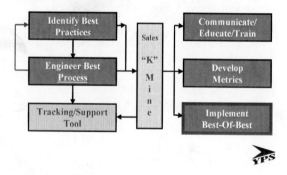

Introduction

Many who have been successful in sales are leery of becoming involved with something that sounds so highly technical and arcane.

To them, "Sales Process Engineering" seems like something that should be restricted to an academic environment or might possibly apply to the "real world", but only for some huge organization. In reality, SPE takes one of the hallmarks of successful selling – **persistence** – and elevates it to a whole new level of effectiveness. It takes the cliché, "plan your work and work your plan," and transforms it from slogan to powerful technique to ensure continuous improvement. It applies to the sales force of thousands, to the "lone ranger" rep of a start-up company and to everyone in between.

Let's take a few steps back. There can be no doubt that Process Engineering principles are proven. GE attributes a savings of $8 billion over the last three years to Six Sigma. ([1] See note) Dow Chemical calculates an average cost reduction $500,000 per project to it. Dell estimates that it took $2.4 million out of its Accounts Payable process. Wellmark reduced the time to add a new doctor to its medical plans from 65+ days to 30 or less,

---

[1] See "Final Thoughts" for a perspective on the importance, significance and value of six sigma for the sales profession.

and was also able to reduce the headcount required to do it. Whether it's Six Sigma, Total Quality Management, Just-In-Time, Mistake-Proofing or any of the other process engineering disciplines, the prodigious contributions to the productivity gains of American business are undeniable.

But Sales is different…

Really? It should, in fact, be surprising (maybe embarrassing?) that sales executives have avoided (resisted?) applying the collective wisdom of Deming, Juran, Hammer, Crosby, Goldratt, Senge, Davenport, etc. If these principles work with near-astonishing effectiveness for Manufacturing, Operations, Administration, Customer Service, Information Technology, Human Resources, Procurement and Logistics, why would it not work for Sales?

Surely, Sales is different. Of all business processes, Sales is the one that most closely approaches "Art" vs. "Science". It truly *is* challenging to apply Process Engineering. That is why the magnitude of the potential competitive advantage from doing it is so compelling.

With Sales Process Engineering, the sales executive can reduce cycle time, wasted time, rework, scrap, work-in-process and the negative impact of dependencies. Constraints can be eliminated. The "Hawthorne Effect" can be harnessed. ([2] See Note) Quality can be increased and best practices, metrics and statistical process control can be exploited.

So how does one get started? First, mentally commit to the continuous implementation of better sales practices. (How can you object to that idea?) Next, recognize the need to maintain that commitment for the remainder of your sales career. Finally, follow an organized process to maximize the efficiency and value of the time you invest in your continuous improvement efforts.

---

[2] A research project at Western Electric's Cicero, IL Hawthorne plant in 1927-32 clearly demonstrated that simply studying a process enhanced the performance of those executing it. When the lighting was made brighter, productivity increased. When a few months later the lights were turned back down... productivity increased again.

Identify Best Practices

The term "Best Practices" often creates mental blocks. When most of us are asked to list a few, we find ourselves groping for profound statements. We want to express deep, original thoughts that will set us apart from our compatriots. As a result, many really good ideas are left unsaid, and worse yet, many reps get turned off to the SPE effort right off the bat.

In practice, it is better to think in terms of a *hierarchy* of practices. Start by seeking out plain old "practices" – things that sales people actually do as part of their day-to-day routine. With a list of sales practices in hand, you can pick out the minority of them that truly are better than the others, i.e., your "Better Practices." Over time, the really effective ones will emerge as "Best Practices"

This hierarchical approach makes it *much* easier to get your SPE initiative started by removing the unrealistic expectation of coming up with *THE* answers immediately. If Sales were that easy, any dummy could do it!

One of the best ways to kick off a SPE project is to ask each sales rep and manager to submit in writing the three things he or she does that contributes most to his or her personal success. What is it? Why does it work? What are the benefits of the practice? Typically, the first time around in this exercise, the practices listed will tend to focus on attitudes (vs. behaviors) and to be somewhat vague. That's OK. Attitudes *are* important and the migration to more concrete, repeatable practices will happen quite quickly.

It is also important to solicit input from all members of the sales force and not limit it to the better performing reps and mangers. Great ideas sometimes come from unexpected places and you never know when a "missing link" concept will come from an inexperienced or low-producing rep. Along the same line of thinking, make extensive use of outside sources as well. Look outside of your own firm, at competitors and even other industries.

Engineer Best Process

A genuine transformation in the effectiveness of Best Practices can occur by engineering them into a "Best Process." (By the way, the same idea of process, better process, best process applies.) There is a profound difference between a set of best practices and a best process.

Remember the Thanksgiving dinner analogy. You could follow a cookbook, a set of best practices, and produce a perfect turkey, perfect stuffing, perfect mashed potatoes, etc. It is another matter entirely to have a *process* to ensure that each component of the meal is ready at the same time! Ever have the turkey ready before the potatoes are peeled? Ever leave out the secret ingredient for the stuffing because you were rushing to get it finished on time?

Using something like the YPS *Methodical Sales Process* (described in a later section) as a baseline, you can arrange practices into their most logical, most effective sequence. With a process, you can better coordinate members of the sales team and support staff. You can avoid situations where, for example, the proposal is ready to go and the customer is waiting, but the pricing has not been finalized or approved.

An even greater value is the ability to more easily isolate the exact portions of your sales cycle that are the sources of the most trouble. These trouble spots, once clearly identified, can be addressed and fixed. (A more thorough discussion of constraints, dependencies, rework, etc. is contained in the Process Engineering – Round 2" chapter.)

Documentation – The Sales Knowledge Mine

__Write it down!__ Documentation is the key enabler and energizer of the whole SPE process. The discipline of documentation forces clarity and completeness. We have all experienced the phenomenon of having what seems to be a breakthrough insight only to realize its flaws as we attempt to explain its value to others.

Even worse and far too often, a forceful speaker will convince a group that a mediocre practice is essential. That same forceful speaker might also win an argument with incomplete or flawed logic. More harm than good flows from a decision to implement mediocre practices and/or apply incomplete, flawed logic.

Repeatability is the key for any process. Unless the practice or process can be written down and then survive the scrutiny of skeptical readers and doers, it cannot legitimately be labeled as "Best."

The detail documentation for each major process step should include three sections. The first section contains clearly stated completion criteria. The next consists of a list of best practices that can or should be executed to accomplish that step. The third section consists of metrics to provide a means to keep score on how well a rep or sales unit is executing that stage of the sales process. A simplified example for the step "Gain Prospect Attention" follows:

❖ Completion Criteria – A face-to-face sales call regarding this opportunity has been scheduled

❖ Best Practices

- ➤ Mail or e-mail an introductory letter
- ➤ Provide a quantified reference from the prospect's industry
- ➤ Conduct basic research and become familiar with the prospect's company and industry
- ➤ Follow-up via telephone to schedule a meeting

- ❖ Metrics – 10 Face-To-Face sales calls per week for new opportunities

Each step of your sales process needs to be documented in this fashion, albeit in substantially more detail. In addition, the entire process needs to be flowcharted. This provides an easy way to visualize how all the steps contribute to the overall success of the sales effort. An example of a "Cross-Functional Flowchart" is contained in Appendix IV.

Documentation requires constant updating. The business environment constantly changes; therefore the sales process must constantly change to accommodate the differences and remain effective. If your sales force has any smarts at all, it is fountain of new ideas and new best practices. These new insights must be continuously fed into the documentation so that they can be applied quickly and broadly.

The final key point with regard to documentation – and this goes hand-in-hand with updating - is availability. Perhaps it goes without saying, but all documentation should be electronically stored and remotely accessible. Put it on your intranet!

Communicate/Educate/Train

Providing continuously updated, easily accessible documentation is only the first part of the "Communicate" job. Sales management must also set a strong expectation that all sales reps consistently and actively use the Sales Knowledge Mine. It must become a "living/growing/evolving" body of knowledge and information. It should be positioned as *the* source of sales and sales process information. "If it's in the mine, there's no excuse for not knowing about it."

The Sales Knowledge mine must also be a two-way street. A "Sales Forum" or bulletin board where anyone can post a question or a comment in response to one should accompany it. This forum must be monitored. Good ideas found here are Best Practice candidates. It is also a great way for sales management to keep a finger on the pulse of what is going on in the field.

The need for education and training regarding the sales process and its effective use should be obvious. Why go through all the effort of designing, building and improving it, if nobody knows what works consistently or how to use the Knowledge Mine to learn more about it? On the flip side, management should also solicit feedback regarding the value and ease-of-use of both the process and the mine.

Finally, here's a related best practice. At least once a year, each rep should be required to conduct a formal, 30-minute sales training session for the entire team. Since the peer group is far and away the toughest audience anyone can face, all the basic sales skills will get tested during the session. Also, since everyone wants to appear to be "top shelf" when on such public display, you ensure a constant flow of new, good ideas that in turn can be fed into the Sales Knowledge Mine.

Develop Metrics

"If it's not measured, it's not managed." W. Edwards Deming, the father of the modern quality movement states it even more plainly, *"What gets measured, gets done."*
Developing metrics is therefore a critical, integral part of the Sales Process Engineering process.

The vast majority of sales organizations have defined only one or two measurements for sales reps. Revenue and gross profit are the most common. Clearly, these are essential, but unless total sales volume *always* exceeds forecast, they are inadequate. Initially, work to define five or six key metrics. These might include number of potential opportunities identified, number of face-to-face calls scheduled and executed each week, number of opportunities where customer personnel are committed to and actively engaged in evaluating your product/service and number of proposals submitted/presented per month along with revenue and profit. As a rule of thumb, define at least one metric for each completion criterion in each step of your sales process.

Over time, as more and more of the steps in your sales process become quickly repeatable, you will find other metrics that are good indicators of a sales process being well executed. Do not be surprised if you find as many as 25, 30 or more.

Implement!!!

Unless the processes, tools, techniques and metrics that result from your sales process engineering are actually used by all members of your sales team – the effort is wasted. How many times have you thought of, heard of or witnessed a great idea in action, and then never implemented it yourself? (Ouch!)

Always using your metrics is the best way to ensure implementation of best practices and best process. *The current status of each rep for each metric with a comparison to standard must be available at all times*.

Re-read the preceding paragraph three times.

Tracking/Support Tool

Information Technology tools are essential for efficient management of a sales process. It involves way too much to keep in your head. The key point to remember is that only *after* processes and metrics have been defined, can appropriate tracking and support tools be effectively selected and implemented. Upwards of 70% of CRM (Customer Relationship Management and SFA (Sales Force Automation) project fail. The most common reason for failure is inadequate definition of the results expected from the use of the system.

Chapter 5 - The Sales Excellence Council

The most effective way to execute and reap the benefits of a Sales Process Engineering effort is to assemble the best and brightest of your sales reps and managers into a professionally facilitated Sales Excellence Council or SEC. Beware, however, because it is a lot tougher to execute and sustain than it sounds.

The Rules

First of all, there are a few rules that all SECs **must** follow…

Rule number one: *Members must be predominantly, if not exclusively, doers*. They need to be card-carrying, responsible-for-meeting-quota reps, managers and executives. (The only partial exception is the facilitator. More on that person shortly) Staff and "outside experts" can be excellent resources, but serve the group best as guests that are invited to participate periodically.

Rule number two: *Prepare yourself and other executives to hear all kinds of things you might not want to hear.* Pet programs and traditions will get challenged. Sacred cows will become burgers. You'll get an overdose of outside-the-box thinking. In other words, be careful what you wish for, especially in light of rule number three, which states...

Rule number three: *Give the group power.* If you inhibit the group - overtly or subtly – from implementing its programs and ideas, you just killed it. From the outset, position membership on the council as an honor, something that your reps aspire to achieve. If a person has not earned the respect of management and peers, he or she should not be nominated for membership. It is also a good idea to appoint members for a term of one or two years. That way, nobody gets burned out and "mistakes" can be removed without too much fanfare.

Rule number four: *Commit to your Sales Excellence council for the long term.* I apologize in advance for the coming cliché, but... Nothing valuable is easy and quick. A Sales Excellence Council is responsible for improving the toughest business process there is – finding, landing and growing those things (called customers) that pay everybody else's salary. If your company is not constantly and forever getting better at it, at least one competitor will. Given rule number five, the long term commitment should not be a problem.

Rule number five: *Set an expectation that the SEC will improve the company's sales process so that the process itself drives an 8-12% annual growth rate.* It is critical that the Council understands that this expected sales growth is *incremental*. In other words, 8-12% above and beyond what you would achieve due to things like a strengthening economy or new products or an acquisition. That's a tall order.

The Tactics

There really is nothing all that complicated about running a Sales Excellence Council. The strategy of the group is to execute Sales Process Engineering. Beyond that, simply apply all of the usual meeting management guidelines. Maintain laser-beam focus on the objective, have agendas pre-published, ensure consistent participation and preparation and maintain good documentation.

A kickoff of one or two full days should consist of an emphatic statement of the objective (8-12% incremental, annual increase in sales per rep), education (regarding Sales Process Engineering, the Methodical Sales Process and the tools to be used) and the initial identification and mapping of Sales Best Practices. After that, a two to four hour monthly meeting works most effectively.

The SEC concept can be applied across a wide variety of organizations regardless of their size and nature. At its most fundamental level, it can be applied at an individual level. It can be scaled up to address a local sales team and/or one that is regional, national or global. An SEC can be fully contained within one corporation or can be sponsored by an industry association with members drawn from multiple companies. Any group with a common set of interests and target markets can work.

Technology is also important. Travel can become an expensive burden. While the kickoff meeting should be a face-to-face affair, follow up meetings can be conducted via web conferencing. In these conferences, all participants link up electronically not only for audio, but also for PC to PC communications. With these capabilities the facilitator/note-taker's screen can be viewed by all attendees regardless of their physical location.

To get an SEC started, use of an "outside expert" to facilitate is advisable. This "SPE Czar" must have executive level sales management experience, a thorough understanding of process engineering principles, project and meeting management skills and working knowledge of the required documentation, diagramming and statistical tools. Once the group is up and running, you may decide to turn this responsibility over to one of your sales leaders or even rotate the job among the key members of the council.

Chapter 6 - The Methodical Sales Process

Every organization is unique. Every organization's sales process has unique aspects. Despite that, however, the overall sales process structure across different companies and industries is quite similar. The YPS Methodical Sales Process (MSP) was designed to exploit this overall similarity and to provide a well-organized, intuitive, logical framework. Because of this, it can serve as not only as a "stake-in-the-ground-starting-point" for a Sales Process Engineering (SPE) effort; it can also provide a basis for sales process quality benchmarking.

The MSP architecture includes fourteen sales sub-processes that are grouped into three main categories... *Sales Operations*, the starting point and "guts" of the whole selling process; *Customer Satisfaction*, concerned with maintaining/enhancing the satisfaction of the current customer base and building credibility with prospects; and *Sales Support*, the activities performed by field reps, staff and management to make the sales operation as productive as possible.

Each of the fourteen sub-processes is further broken down into four parts; Completion Criteria, Metrics, Best Practices and Tools. Completion Criteria unambiguously define conditions that exist when a sub-process has been completed. For example, you might define completion of the "Identity Opportunities" sub-process as having the decision maker's name and contact information.

Methodical Sales Process

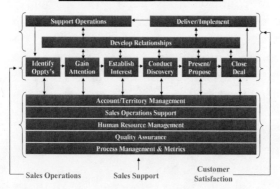

Metrics provide a means to keep score. They are the quantitative, non-debatable aspect of how well a sub-process is being executed. For example, you may decide that for your business, each sales rep must have a minimum of 50 opportunities that meet the completion criteria for the "Identify Opportunities" sub-process.

Sales Best Practices are the most effective activities and tasks that must be executed to complete a sub-process. Note that "best" is a relative term. It may be helpful to think in terms of practices, good practices, better practices and ultimately best practices. Start by documenting what you and your team actually do. Over time, you can eliminate the time spent executing "good" practices and focus on only the "best" ones. As you would expect, the list of practices for any sub-process continuously changes as your customers, competitors and market conditions change.

Tools are exactly what they sound like, prospect lists, sample value propositions, product samples, brochures, pricing tools, proposal boilerplate, references… All those things that can be used to help advance a sale.

Send an e-mail to info@ypsgroup.com to get a blank MSP in MS Word format.

What follows is a brief description of each of the fourteen sub-processes in the YPS MSP. Sample completion criteria, metrics and practices are provided. *Note that while the sub-processes are applicable to companies in virtually all industries, the completion criteria, metrics and best practices may vary by industry.*

Sales Operations

Identify Opportunities

❖ Completion Criteria
  ➢ Opportunity information entered into the CRM data base
  ➢ Decision maker's contact information entered into CRM data base

❖ Metrics
  ➢ Number of opportunities at this stage
  ➢ Identified potential revenue
  ➢ % of Identify stage prospects moved to "Gain Attention"
  ➢ Days to move "Identify" stage prospects moved to "Gain Attention"

- ❖ Best Practices
  - ➤ Segment current customer base by industry, size, growth rate, profitability, etc. to determine likely characteristics of a "good" prospect
  - ➤ Ask current customers about potential future requirements
  - ➤ Use internet tools & data bases to identity account names and individual prospects
  - ➤ Call prospect companies to identify decision makers
  - ➤ Ask current contacts for references inside and outside his/her company

- ❖ Tools
  - ➤ Hoovers.com
  - ➤ EDGAR
  - ➤ Chamber of Commerce listings

Gain Attention

- ❖ Completion Criteria
  - ➤ First face-to-face call with the decision maker is scheduled

- ❖ Metrics
  - ➤ Number of opportunities at this stage
  - ➤ Potential revenue at this stage by prospect
  - ➤ % of "Gain Attention" stage prospects moved to "Establish Interest"
  - ➤ Days to move "Gain Attention" stage prospects moved to "Establish Interest"

- ❖ Best Practices
  - ➤ Carefully script and rehearse, rehearse, rehearse the following:
    - ▪ One sentence value statement (Why they should meet with you)
    - ▪ For each target market segment - "Elevator Pitch" (90 second statement of your value and why they should meet with you)
      - • Telephone version
      - • Voice Mail version
      - • Face-To-Face version
  - ➤ Cold call the prospect
  - ➤ Send direct mail or e-mail piece with applicable reference and quantified value to decision maker, then call for appointment
  - ➤ Get a reference (or someone who knows the decision maker) to call the

decision maker to recommend a meeting. Follow-up to schedule
- ➤ Publish articles in appropriate trade magazines, web sites, etc. Include your contact information
- ➤ Speak at local events
- ➤ Attend "networking" meetings regularly

- ❖ Tools
  - ➤ Scripted cold calls
  - ➤ Value Statement samples

Establish Interest

- ❖ Completion Criteria
  - ➤ Decision maker is committed to *DO SOMETHING* (e.g., follow-up meeting, reference site visit, set up meeting with subordinates or other executive)
  - ➤ Action plan with dates is entered into the CRM data base

- ❖ Metrics
  - ➤ Number of opportunities at this stage
  - ➤ Potential revenue at this stage by prospect

- ➢ % of "Establish Interest" stage prospects moved to "Discovery"
- ➢ Days to move "Establish Interest" stage prospects moved to "Discovery"

- ❖ Best Practices
  - ➢ Carefully script and rehearse, rehearse, rehearse a standardized version of a "Killer Introductory Sales Call" for each target market segment and level of executive
    - ▪ Use specific references
    - ▪ Use verifiable, quantified value statements
  - ➢ Document a "Call Plan" for every call that customizes the standard call as needed
  - ➢ Use a set of high-quality sales aids & tools
  - ➢ Be prepared with appropriate "leave behind" material
  - ➢ Always make the first call with a partner (e.g., tech support rep, sales manager)
  - ➢ Document the call results including all "TODOs" and due dates– get it to the decision maker within 24 hours

- ❖ Tools
  - ➤ Key questions to ask
  - ➤ Sample action plans – Best/2nd Best/Minimal

Conduct Discovery

- ❖ Completion Criteria
  - ➤ Customer requirements document is complete and confirmed by customer
  - ➤ Internal "Solution Phase Quality Assurance review is completed
  - ➤ Client Decision Process & Criteria Identified, Documented and Agreed to
  - ➤ Decision Maker Committed to Attend Proposal Presentation
  - ➤ CRM data base updated

- ❖ Metrics
  - ➤ Number of opportunities at this stage
  - ➤ Potential revenue at this stage by prospect
  - ➤ % of "Discovery" stage prospects moved to "Present/Propose"
  - ➤ Days to move "Discovery" stage prospects moved to "Present/Propose"

❖ Best Practices
  ➢ Conduct requirements study – verify results with decision maker
  ➢ Conduct customer executive briefing(s)
  ➢ Conduct product/service education session(s) for decision influencers
  ➢ Determine and document the customer's decision process and criteria, including identity of decision-maker and influencers
  ➢ Verify "conditional" or "preliminary" support from decision-maker and influencers

❖ Tools
  ➢ Total Cost of Ownership data collection & calculation spreadsheet
  ➢ Proposal content checklist
  ➢ Common decision criteria & calculator

Present/Propose

❖ Completion Criteria
  ➢ Formal or informal proposal submitted and/or formal presentation of recommendations to decision maker completed

- ➢ CRM data base updated

- ❖ Metrics
  - ➢ Number of opportunities at this stage
  - ➢ Potential revenue at this stage by prospect
  - ➢ % of "Present/Propose" stage prospects moved to "Close"
  - ➢ Days to move "Present/Propose" stage prospects moved to "Close"

- ❖ Best Practices
  - ➢ Always submit a written proposal for ALL opportunities
  - ➢ Use standardized proposal format and boilerplate – ALWAYS include a customer signoff/commitment page
  - ➢ Hand deliver the proposal to the decision maker and key decision influencers
  - ➢ Ensure that the decision maker is available and attends entire proposal presentation – reschedule if necessary

- ❖ Tools
  - ➢ Boilerplate
  - ➢ Product/service spec sheets

Close

❖ Completion Criteria
  ➤ Customer has paid the first invoice in full

❖ Metrics
  ➤ Number of opportunities at this stage
  ➤ Potential revenue at this stage by prospect
  ➤ % Closed
  ➤ Days to Close

❖ Best Practices
  ➤ Ask for the order at the beginning (and if necessary, the close) of the formal proposal presentation
  ➤ Fully document all objections, their background and how they are resolved (or not resolved)
  ➤ Send a "decision announcement" to all involved customer personnel with 24 hours of the "go-ahead"

Customer Satisfaction

Deliver/Implement

❖ Completion Criteria
  ➢ Customer has signed off on delivery/implementation

❖ Metrics – Obtain customer signoff for 100% of implementations

❖ Best Practices
  ➢ Formally review delivery/implementation checklist with customer
  ➢ Develop and review "Implementation Issues" document – take appropriate action to prevent future problems

Support Customer Operations

❖ Completion Criteria
  ➢ KAPS review submitted to customer annually (Key Account Performance Summary – see http://www.ypsgroup.com/december2 002.htm)

- ➢ Customer Satisfaction review/survey completed annually

- ❖ Metrics – 100% of customers rated at "Good" or better customer satisfaction

- ❖ Best Practices
  - ➢ Prepare and submit an annual KAPS report (Key Account Performance Summary – see http://www.ypsgroup.com/december2002.htm)
  - ➢ Conduct a customer satisfaction survey at least annually
  - ➢ Conduct a Customer Focus survey
  - ➢ Conduct monthly/quarterly performance reviews with customer
  - ➢ Jointly with each customer, develop key performance metrics and continuously monitor them

Develop Relationships

- ❖ Completion Criteria
  - ➢ Quality of all key contacts at all key customers are rated as "A" (see http://www.ypsgroup.com/december2001.htm)

❖ Metrics
  - ➢ 33% of contacts rated as "A"
  - ➢ 25% of all "C" contacts upgraded to "B" annually
  - ➢ 25% of all "B" contacts upgraded to "A" annually

❖ Best Practices
  - ➢ Formally rate your relationships with contacts at least annually
  - ➢ Implement and execute a process to ensure 100% follow-up on your commitments to customers
  - ➢ Provide a continuous stream of *relevant, useful* information to contacts
  - ➢ Use a variety of "touch base" techniques (e-mail, voice mail, drop by, etc.) – use them all, but predominantly the one each contact prefers
  - ➢ Conduct monthly "no surprises" reviews with key contacts
  - ➢ Regularly attend social, sporting and other events with key customers
  - ➢ Take a customer to breakfast/lunch/dinner
  - ➢ Operate a Customer Advisory Council

Sales Support

NOTE: Sales Support consists of a series of back-office/staff functions. There is great variability by industry in the types and priorities of required activities. For the most part therefore, only sample Best Practices are listed. As these are developed for your own company, specific completion criteria, metrics and tools should be defined for each Sales Support Best Practice.

Account & Territory Management

❖ Best Practices
  ➢ Maintain a rolling 12 month forecast of business by segment, customer/prospect and opportunity – update it monthly
  ➢ Conduct formal, annual Account Planning sessions with monthly or quarterly informal updates (Each Rep must have a documented Account/Territory plan that has been formally updated within 90 days)
  ➢ Develop and implement a coverage strategy to ensure consistent contact with key decision makers and influencers

- ➢ Keep the CRM data base updated constantly – use it consistently
- ➢ Consistently use a Sales Force Automation (SFA) system to ensure follow-up on all commitments
- ➢ Be aware of and use all available support resources – Keep track of what you use, where and how well it worked
- ➢ Track "Customer Share" for all key accounts (Customer Share is like market share, but focused on a single customer)
- ➢ Maintain a formal customer retention strategy and tactical plan
- ➢ Formally review performance against all key metrics monthly
- ➢ Use various sales channels for some/all of the sales process

Field Operations Support

- ❖ Best Practices
  - ➢ Segment the market
    - ▪ Classify all accounts and prospects according to appropriate criteria (e.g., industry, revenue, potential revenue, growth, profitability, etc.)

- Collect & analyze both internal sales data & public data bases
- Identify business issues and requirements for each segment
- ➢ Maintain a "Product/Service to Customer Matrix" (to identify cross-selling opportunities)
- ➢ Conduct Product Marketing
  - Provide for easy access to product/service sales support personnel that are both technically and application knowledgeable
  - Maintain a library of references
  - Maintain a library of product/services application descriptions
  - Collect, maintain and prioritize product requirements based on customer & sales rep feedback
- ➢ Provide proposal boilerplate and preparation support
- ➢ Maintain library of company and product/service information (electronic and paper)
  - Company value statement(s)
  - Company differentiators
  - Brochures – Somewhat detailed product/service descriptions -

> > Highly detailed technical
> > specifications
> - Develop a clear pricing strategy along
>   with an exception-handling process
> - Conduct competitive research and
>   analysis
> - Provide Information Technology
>   Support
>   - Operate a CRM/SFA system
>   (Customer Relationship
>   Management/Sales Force
>   Automation)
>   - Maintain a high quality web site
>   - Provide cell phones, laptops and
>   other tools
> - Conduct regular/periodic promotional
>   campaigns

Human Resources

- ❖ Best Practices
  - Formalize the
    recruiting/screening/hiring process
  - Develop, maintain and use a "new
    sales rep" training curriculum
  - Conduct product, service and
    professional sales training regularly

- ➢ Conduct job and employee profiling –
  ensure a match between job
  requirements and individuals
- ➢ Develop a sales compensation plan
  that matches closely with company
  requirements – administer it fairly and
  consistently
- ➢ Implement written performance plans
  for each sales rep – Conduct informal
  quarterly and formal annual
  performance reviews

Quality Assurance

- ❖ Best Practices
  - ➢ Conduct "War Room Meetings" for all
    significant opportunities at appropriate
    checkpoints including pre-proposal –
    All affected sales and support
    personnel and management should
    attend
  - ➢ Conduct regular Win & Loss Reviews
    to identify what does and does not
    work
  - ➢ Conduct a "CPA" (Customer
    Perception Audit) for all key accounts
    annually (see
    http://www.ypsgroup.com/cpa.htm)

Process Management & Metrics

- ❖ Best Practices
  - ➤ Appoint a "SPE Czar" – i.e., an individual with responsibility for documentation of, training/education on and continuous improvement of your sales process
  - ➤ Involve top sales performers in the continuous improvement & development of the sales process
  - ➤ Develop and maintain quantitative measurements for all significant sales activities
    - Funnel
    - Account Importance (how well it fits the definition of the "perfect' customer/prospect)
    - Relationship Quality
  - ➤ Integrate automated tracking and analysis of these metrics in the CRM system

Chapter 7 - Process Engineering Round 2

Chapter 4 described the basics of process engineering. This chapter will briefly review a number of additional concepts that are important contributors to sustaining continuous improvement. They are all factors that need to be measured. Keep in mind that the process of process engineering, like any other process needs its own metrics.

Constraints

A constraint is something – anything – that slows down or stops progress through a process. Constraints need to be identified, defined and prioritized. Next they need to be addressed, alleviated or removed by the sales rep and/or team.

Some constraints will be immediately obvious to your Sales Excellence Council. They might, in fact, already be obvious. Therein lays the danger. Don't assume that the easily observable constraints are the *key* constraints. Sales people especially, with their instinctive bias to action, have a strong tendency to leap into "fix-it mode," and might well expend substantial energy attacking a secondary problem.

The vast majority of the *key* constraints will not be identified so easily. It will first be necessary to define the overall sales process, define performance standards and metrics for each major step, collect actual performance data, analyze it, set priorities and then act. Arm yourself with the facts before committing valuable resources.

Also, be aware of and don't get frustrated by the one immutable law of constraints. As quickly as you find and fix one key constraint, another one pops up in an unexpected place. Sales Process Engineering ends only when all the constraints to selling more have been eliminated. In other words, **never**. It's simply the nature of a firm commitment to continuous improvement.

Dependencies

A dependency is a special type of constraint that results from the need to have something done/delivered by another person, department, or company. It's not enough to know only your own process. Others on whom you depend must know it too, and it's *you* that needs to make sure they know it. Not in as much detail, but enough to know that when X happens, they need to start working on A so that when you get finished doing Y, they'll have completed B so that you can deliver C to the tech support rep so he can take the C and Y to accomplish Z (Yes, it *does* get that complex!)

The mirror image of the above is also true. You as the sales rep or manager need an appreciation of other people's processes, *especially* those of your customers.

Rework

Do it right the first time. The cost of doing something for the second time is *far* more expensive than doing it the first time. For example, assume a rep entered the wrong "bill to" address on an order. While it only took a few seconds for him to enter the wrong information and just another few seconds to correct the order, think of what else happened.

The customer wasted time contacting your Accounts Receivable department to point out the mistake. You're A/R person wasted time identifying and then tracking down the rep to point out the error and ask him to correct it. The Billing department wasted time sending out a new invoice and the customer wasted time processing it – again.

Meanwhile, your Finance department had to re-do their cash flow analysis because the expected receipt from that customer did not arrive. And then… And then… And then… You get the point.

Never underestimate the magnitude of the ripple effect caused by rework.

Work In Process (WIP)

In sales, Work-In-Process consists of all the opportunities in your sales funnel or pipeline. Is it possible to have too many opportunities? The knee-jerk answer is, "No," but in reality the opposite is true.

Let's say that you have been really focused on working ten specific opportunities. Closing three of them will put you over quota. You've worked hard, finished up "Discovery" of customer requirements for all ten and all that's needed now is a well-written proposal for each. Since you did such a great job of creating customer enthusiasm, all ten want their proposals by Friday. The technical support you need to create the documentation can get two of them completed in time. Oops!

Because you didn't consider the well-known constraints and dependencies, you find yourself with too much WIP at the "Proposal" stage of your funnel. Several of the deals will probably fall through because of long proposal turn-around time.

Here's the point. Figure out the capacity at each stage of the sales process. Know the optimal number of opportunities for each stage and work to maintain balance. For example, You need to close 5 deals each month, so you need to deliver10 proposals per month, which means you need 20 deals in the "Discovery" stage at all times and therefore 50 at the "Interest" stage.

Cycle Time

How long is your sell cycle? It's an innocuous question that shockingly few sales reps and managers can answer with anything beyond a wild guess. It is, however, arguably *the* most important sales metric.

First, foremost and obviously, shortening the sell cycle enables a greater number of cycles in any given time period and therefore results in more total sales. Less time required also means a lower sales cost per dollar of revenue. In other words, a detailed understanding of cycle time means not only more revenue, but also a greater profit margin.

Think about breaking cycle time down into its component parts. How much time does each stage of the sales funnel require? Find the longest stage and focus on reducing it. For each stage, how much of the total cycle time is spent working and how much time is spent waiting for something? A high wait to work time ratio indicates that a significant constraint and/or dependency is present or that there is too much work in process. At what point does your wait to work ratio become too high? Do you know?

Cycle time is one of those things that becomes more and more valuable the more you think about. The more you know about it – i.e., the quantitative detail for each sales task including how long, how much and the wait/work ratio – the more you can think about it. *If you do nothing else with regard to Sales Process Engineering, become an expert regarding the details of your sales cycle time.*

Yield

Knowing the yield percentage for each rep on your team for each stage of the sales funnel is an extremely powerful means to identify best practices. For example, say on average that 50% of your company's proposals result in a sale. Looking at the yield statistics shows that 80% of Ed's proposals are winners. Without a doubt, Ed is doing something different and better. Find out what it is and teach it to Amy, whose yield is only 20%.

The stats may also show that Amy gets 60% of her "Interest" stage opportunities to move along to the "Discovery" stage in 15 days. Ed only gets 30% and it takes him 45 days. In other words, Ed and Amy have much to teach each other. In any sales force, different people are good at different things. Find out who is best at what and have that person share best practices with everyone else on the team. (Also, note the added insight provided by combining yield data with cycle time data in the last example.)

Appendix I - SPE Tools

One piece of good news is that the software packages needed to support a Sales Process Engineering effort are all fairly standard. Following is the list of software normally used by The YPS Group in its SPE engagements:

- Word – for the obvious uses.

- Excel – again for the obvious uses. Unless you have looked, you may not realize the wide array of quite powerful statistical analysis functions contained in this program.

- Access – for data storage and report generation. This is a basic, yet powerful relational data base.

- FrontPage – for web development. Our Sales Knowledge Mines are built using this tool. If you already know Word, you can be building basic web sites in about two hours.

- Visio – for diagramming like Cross Functional Flow Charts, Entity-Relationship Diagrams, etc. A bit challenging to learn, but worth the effort in time saved creating diagrams.

- Snitz – for online forums and bulletin boards. It's good and it's free! http://forum.snitz.com/

- Acrobat – for easy distribution of all documentation.

Appendix II - A shameless sales pitch

Yes, I know that a book is not an appropriate place for sales pitch. But… I'm a salesman and just can't help myself.

As a sales manager or executive, you should consider engaging The YPS Group to get your team started down the path of Sales Process Engineering. Can you really afford to ignore the possibility of generating an 8-12% annual, incremental increase in sales performance?

SPE is my favorite subject and I love to think, talk and correspond about it. My partners and I are easy to contact:

- Call: 770-514-1189

- E-mail: todd@ypsgroup.com

- Visit our Sales Forum, ask a question, add your two cents or just read.
  http://ypsgroup.com/forums/default.asp

- Surf around our web site.
  www.ypsgroup.com

- Subscribe to "Ideas!" Our free takes-less-than-a-minute-to-read monthly e-newsletter is designed to get you thinking about how to sell more faster. Send an e-mail to subscribe@ypsgroup.com

Appendix III – The President's Model

The President's Model

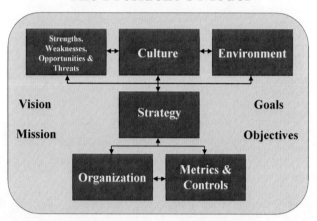

The following pages contain a "fill-in-the-blanks" copy of the YPS President's Model. A Microsoft Word version is available upon e-mail request to info@ypsgroup.com.

The President's Model is an excellent guide for developing a strategic plan. It should be reviewed regularly and updated annually. All functions and levels in the firm should be involved. Versions of it should be completed for the firm as a whole and for each major functional area.

Company Name: _____

President's Model

Vision

❖ A one-sentence statement that provides a broad, long-term summary of what the firm is striving to become.

❖ For example: IVANS Inc.'s vision is to be the predominant pathway for electronic commerce, serving the insurance and healthcare industries.

❖ Your vision:

_____

_____

_____

_____

_____

_____

Mission

❖ A one-sentence statement of what the firm intends to achieve for it's customers and how.

❖ For example: Improve the profit performance and productivity of our members and their trading partners through the efficient acquisition and strategic application of communications and information technologies.

❖ Your mission:

_____
_____
_____
_____
_____
_____
_____
_____
_____
_____
_____

<u>Goals</u>

❖ Three to five broad, one-sentence statements that describe the key things that will be accomplished to achieve the vision and mission.

❖ For example:

> ➢ Grow the interface business
> ➢ Develop Electronic Commerce Solutions and Services
> ➢ Develop Consultative partnerships with members to advance their business progress
> ➢ Continue to build communities of common interest

❖ Your goals:

> ➢ _____
> _____
> _____
> _____
> _____

Objectives

❖ Three to five statements of specific targets to be met. Each must answer the question, "How much, by when?" This page should be completed for the firm as a whole and for each major department.

❖ For example:

  ➢ Achieve revenue of $50 Million in 2001.
  ➢ Earn 27% net profit before tax over the next three years.
  ➢ Develop three new products/services that contribute $2 Million in annual revenue by year-end 2005.
  ➢ Increase productivity (revenue per employee) by 10% by year-end 2002.

❖ Your objectives:

  ➢ _____
    _____
    _____
    _____
    _____

➢ _____
  _____
  _____
  _____
  _____

➢ _____
  _____
  _____
  _____
  _____

➢ _____
  _____
  _____
  _____
  _____

➢ _____
  _____
  _____
  _____
  _____

Environment

❖ A series of statements regarding significant factors affecting the business over which the firm has no control. These could be regarding social, political, macro-economic, market and/or other factors.

❖ For example:

> ➤ Tight and rapidly changing regulation by federal and state governments
> ➤ Extremely low unemployment
> ➤ Entry of multiple foreign firms into the U.S.
> ➤ Intense merger/acquisition activity

❖ Your key environmental factors:

> ➤ _____
>   _____
>   _____
>
> ➤ _____
>   _____
>   _____

➢ _____
_____
_____
_____

➢ _____
_____
_____
_____

➢ _____
_____
_____
_____

➢ _____
_____
_____
_____

➢ _____
_____
_____
_____

➢ _____
_____
_____
_____

➢ _____
_____
_____
_____

Culture

❖ Companies vary substantially across a wide range of formal and informal variables that reflect aspects of corporate culture. Some of these aspects can be seen in the way companies perform certain functions, others in prevalent attitudes and modes of behavior and others in some of the operating activities and results of the company.

❖ Circle the most appropriate number for your firm:

➢ Personnel

- Turnover ....….. Tenure
  - 1   2   3   4   5

- New hires at all levels …………...
  ……. New hires at entry level only
  - 1   2   3   4   5

- Money = Security ……………..
  ………... = Lifetime employment
  - 1   2   3   4   5

- ▪ Discrete Contract …
  … Loyalty, Membership
  - • 1   2   3   4   5

- ➢ Social responsibility

  - ▪ Profit Maximization …
    … Good Corporate Citizen
    - • 1   2   3   4   5

- ➢ Power Relationships

  - ▪ Strong superior/weak subordinate
    … Collegial
    - • 1   2   3   4   5

  - ▪ Formal Hierarchy…
    … Informal
    - • 1   2   3   4   5

  - ▪ Closed Policy Forums …
    …Open Policy Forums
    - • 1   2   3   4   5

  - ▪ Vertical Communications…
    …Horizontal Communications
    - • 1   2   3   4   5

- Individual Authority …
  … Group Authority
  - 1   2   3   4   5

- Single Decision-Maker …
  …Group Decision Making
  - 1   2   3   4   5

- Survival of the Fittest …
  … Parliamentary
  - 1   2   3   4   5

> Manager's Role

- Financial Manager …
  … Entrepreneur
  - 1   2   3   4   5

- Watch Dog ……………… Gardener
  - 1   2   3   4   5

- Explicit/Discrete Objectives …
  … Implicit/Broad Objectives
  - 1   2   3   4   5

- Controls

  - Direct ....……..... Indirect
    - 1   2   3   4   5

  - Strong ....….... Weak
    - 1   2   3   4   5

  - Formal .... Informal
    - 1   2   3   4   5

- Performance Evaluation

  - Formal/Regular …
                … Informal/Periodic
    - 1   2   3   4   5

  - Frequent .... Infrequent
    - 1   2   3   4   5

  - Quantitative & Objective …
          … Qualitative & Subjective
    - 1   2   3   4   5

- Operational Emphasis

  - Efficiency …….......... Excellence
    - 1   2   3   4   5

- Short Term .... Long Term
  - 1   2   3   4   5

- Financial .... Strategic Position
  - 1   2   3   4   5

> Planning

- Tactical .... Strategic
  - 1   2   3   4   5

- Formal/Tight .... Stretch/Creative
  - 1   2   3   4   5

<u>SWOTs</u>

❖ Strengths - Your firm's major pluses

➢ _____
   _____
   _____

➢ _____
   _____
   _____

➢ _____
   _____
   _____

➢ _____
   _____
   _____

➢ _____
   _____
   _____

❖ Weaknesses - Your firm's major minuses

➢ _____
   _____
   _____

➢ _____

_____

_____

_____

➢ _____

_____

_____

_____

➢ _____

_____

_____

_____

➢ _____

_____

_____

_____

❖ Opportunities - Things/situations your firm could exploit

➢ _____

_____

_____

_____

➢ _____

_____

_____

_____

➢ _____
  _____
  _____
  _____

➢ _____
  _____
  _____
  _____

➢ _____
  _____
  _____
  _____

❖ Threats - Things/situations that could hurt your firm

  ➢ _____
    _____
    _____
    _____

  ➢ _____
    _____
    _____
    _____

  ➢ _____
    _____
    _____
    _____

➢ _____
  _____
  _____

➢ _____
  _____
  _____

Strategy

❖ Four to six specific statements of how the firm and each of the major departments will achieve its goals & objectives and fulfill the vision & mission

❖ For example:

  ➢ Finance
    ▪ Assess and reinforce the operating plan process
    ▪ Ensure earlier and more disciplining role in the business development process

  ➢ Information Technology

- Implement a new internet web site with customer order entry capability
- Implement billing system with integrated A/R

> Sales
- Implement quarterly product and selling skills training sessions
- Migrate from product-oriented specialization to customer need-oriented specialization

❖ Strategy for _____:

> _____
_____
_____

> _____
_____
_____

> _____
_____
_____

➢ _____
_____
_____
_____

➢ _____
_____
_____
_____

❖ Strategy for _____ :

➢ _____
_____
_____
_____

➢ _____
_____
_____
_____

➢ _____
_____
_____
_____

➢ _____
_____
_____
_____

➢ _____
_____
_____

❖ Strategy for _____:

➢ _____
_____
_____

➢ _____
_____
_____

➢ _____
_____
_____

➢ _____
_____
_____

➢ _____
_____
_____

❖ Strategy for _____:

> _____
  _____
  _____

> _____
  _____
  _____

> _____
  _____
  _____

> _____
  _____
  _____

> _____
  _____
  _____

❖ Strategy for _____:

> _____
  _____
  _____

➢ _____
_____
_____

➢ _____
_____
_____

➢ _____
_____
_____

➢ _____
_____
_____

❖ Strategy for _____:

➢ _____
_____
_____

➢ _____
_____
_____

➢ _____
_____
_____
_____

➢ _____
_____
_____
_____

➢ _____
_____
_____
_____

❖ Strategy for _____:

➢ _____
_____
_____
_____

➢ _____
_____
_____
_____

➢ _____
_____
_____
_____

> _____
_____
_____
_____

> _____
_____
_____
_____

Organization

- ❖ Insert your organization chart here. Update it at least quarterly.

Measurements

- ❖ Specific definitions of key measurements for the firm and for each major department

- ❖ For example:

  - > Finance
    - Collection period - Average number of days between mailing of invoice to deposit in our bank
    - Closing Report - Percentage of time that monthly financial results

> report is delivered by the third working day of the month

- ➤ Information Technology
  - Percentage of the time between 8:00 a.m. and 5:00 p.m., Monday through Friday that the network is available
  - Percentage of projects that are delivered on time or early and on or under budget
- ➤ Sales
  - Revenue growth - Percentage increase in year-to-date revenue over last year
  - Call Reporting - Percentage of weeks that call reports are complete, accurate and submitted by noon Monday

❖ Key Measurements for _____:

➤ _____
  _____
  _____

➤ _____
  _____
  _____

➢ _____
  _____
  _____
  _____

➢ _____
  _____
  _____
  _____

➢ _____
  _____
  _____
  _____

❖ Key Measurements for _____:

➢ _____
  _____
  _____

➢ _____
  _____
  _____

➢ _____
  _____
  _____

➢ _____
     _____
     _____

➢ _____
     _____
     _____

❖ Key Measurements for _____:

➢ _____
     _____
     _____

➢ _____
     _____
     _____

➢ _____
     _____
     _____

➢ _____
     _____
     _____

➢ _____
     _____
     _____

❖ Key Measurements for _____:

> _____
  _____
  _____

> _____
  _____
  _____

> _____
  _____
  _____

> _____
  _____
  _____

> _____
  _____
  _____

Key Measurements for _____:

> _____
  _____
  _____

- ➢ _____
  _____
  _____
  _____

- ➢ _____
  _____
  _____
  _____

- ➢ _____
  _____
  _____
  _____

- ➢ _____
  _____
  _____
  _____

- ❖ Key Measurements for _____:

  - ➢ _____
    _____
    _____

  - ➢ _____
    _____
    _____

  - ➢ _____
    _____
    _____

> _____
  _____
  _____

> _____
  _____
  _____

❖ Key Measurements for _____:

  > _____
    _____
    _____

  > _____
    _____
    _____

  > _____
    _____
    _____

  > _____
    _____
    _____

Appendix IV – Sample Sales Process Cross-Functional Flowchart

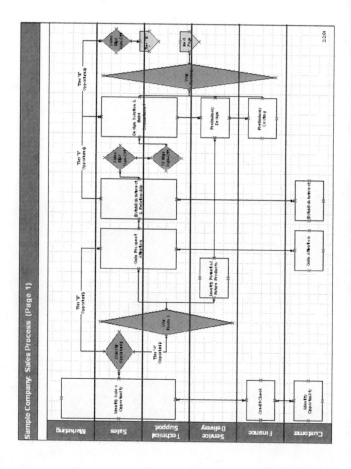

Appendix V – A few useful web sites

❖ www.ypsgroup.com – the web site of The YPS Group, Inc. It contains a wealth of information, links and descriptions of services to implement Sales Process Engineering

❖ www.ypsgroup.com/sbpba - A "semi-secret" web site that provides an overview of an extensive "Sales Best Practices Benchmarking Assessment" conducted by The YPS Group, in the fall of 2003.

❖ www.ypsgroup.com/SellMore.htm - The assessment tool used to gather data for the "SBPBA" project noted above. This is an ongoing project and we would appreciate your input. It takes about 20-25 minutes to complete it.

❖ www.ypsgroup.com/process_assess.htm - A description of a Sales Process Assessment, an excellent first step in a Sales Process Engineering effort.

Final Thoughts… Strive to be a ZERO!!!???

The topic here is the "six sigma" continuous process improvement methodology essentially invented at Motorola, made famous by GE and the subject of many books and articles. Let's end the suspense right now. Any sales rep or team that can achieve _zero_ sigma performance will be immediately entered into the Sales Hall of Fame. Consider the sales funnel below…

The numbers for any given rep in any given company may well be different, but we have found that what is represented here is fairly typical. In this example, the rep has $250 million worth of opportunity in the "Identification" stage of the sales process. On average in this organization, 25% of these opportunities move on to the next stage in about 45 days. This results in $62.5 million in the "Attention" phase, etc.

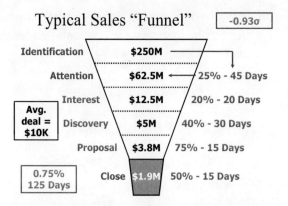

Typical Sales "Funnel"   -0.93σ

Identification	$250M	
Attention	$62.5M	25% - 45 Days
Interest	$12.5M	20% - 20 Days
Discovery	$5M	40% - 30 Days
Proposal	$3.8M	75% - 15 Days
Close	$1.9M	50% - 15 Days

Avg. deal = $10K

0.75% 125 Days

The end result is $1.9 million in sales in 125 days. That means 0.75% of the "suspects" from the Identification stage ultimately turn into orders. Viewed from a six sigma perspective, that is a -0.93 sigma performance.

Yes, it's a negative number!

For a bit more perspective, take a look at the following table. It shows the percentage yield associated with each sigma level.

- 6σ is 99.99966% yield (3.4 errors per million)
- 5σ is 99.977% yield (233 errors per million)
- 4σ is 99.38% yield (6,210 errors per million)
- 3σ is 93.4% yield (67K errors per million)
- 2σ is 69% yield (309K errors per million)
- 1σ is 31% yield (691K errors per million)
- 0σ is 6.7% yield (933K errors per million)
- -0.5σ is 2% yield (988K errors per million)

The next table puts things in a more familiar context. Note that each is an example of *five sigma* performance:

- 1 hour of unsafe drinking water per month
- 2 unsafe landings per day at O'Hare
- 16,000 pieces of lost mail per *hour*
- 500 incorrect surgical operations per week

- 50 newborns dropped by doctors per day
- 22,000 checks deducted from the wrong account per _hour_

Finally, take a look at what the same sales funnel shown above can yield:

- -0.93σ yields $ 1.9 million revenue
- -0.5σ yields $ 5.8 million
- 0σ yields $16.8 million

Strive to be a zero, get there, and you wind up selling almost _nine times_ as much!!!

As a sales executive, manager or professional, does it make sense to learn a bit more about this six sigma stuff??? Well, yes and no. Clearly the magnitude of the potential improvement is gigantic. The problem is, it takes a statistician's mind set, followed by months and months of training to become proficient.

Now the good news. From a six sigma perspective, the typical sales process is so vastly, wildly out of control that just a little bit can go a long way.

Consider Michelangelo and his Pieta, hailed by many to be one of history's finest accomplishments in sculpture. To capture the eerily life-like expressions, he used a fine, soft cloth to "carve" his final touches. Now think about day one of his project. Work started with huge block of solid marble (i.e., a big hunk of stone!!!) and a sledge hammer.

The sales process is still at the sledge hammer stage. There is no need to study and learn the "fine, soft cloth" nuances of six sigma to make really significant progress. Anyone who has gotten this far through this book already knows enough to get started. Sales Process Engineering as I practice it is grounded in six sigma. It follows the "DMAIC" outline: Define – Measure – Analyze – Improve – Control…

- ❖ **Define** - Clearly map out the process to be improved. (The Methodical Sales Process along with the core Sales Practices provide the starting point.)

- ❖ **Measure** - Identify the key measure of effectiveness and efficiency. (See the examples in the "MSP" section of this book.)

❖ **Analyze** - Determine the causes of problem(s). (A spreadsheet program has much more than enough number-crunching power.)

❖ **Improve** - Enhance the performance of the process. (You do get to use your creativity after all!)

❖ **Control** - Ensure that the improvement is sustained over time.

With this DMAIC philosophy in mind, use the SPE concepts contained in this book to Sell More Faster with Sales Process Engineering.

Now…

Go sell more… Sell it faster…